Exploring
Our
Solar System

DWARF PLANETS

Susan Ring and
Alexis Roumanis

www.av2books.com

Step 1

Go to **www.av2books.com**

Step 2

Enter this unique code

YISDRY5WL

Step 3

Explore your interactive eBook!

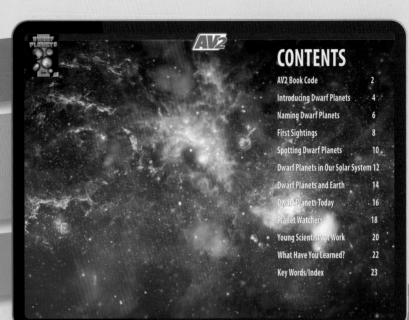

CONTENTS

AV2 is optimized for use on any device

Your interactive eBook comes with...

Contents
Browse a live contents page to easily navigate through resources

Audio
Listen to sections of the book read aloud

Videos
Watch informative video clips

Weblinks
Gain additional information for research

Try This!
Complete activities and hands-on experiments

Key Words
Study vocabulary, and complete a matching word activity

Quizzes
Test your knowledge

Slideshows
View images and captions

... and much, much more!

Exploring
Our
Solar System

DWARF PLANETS

CONTENTS

Introducing
Dwarf Planets

Planets are one group of objects in the **solar system**. Two other groups of objects can also be found in the solar system. These are dwarf planets and small solar system bodies, such as **asteroids**. The five known dwarf planets in Earth's solar system are Ceres, Pluto, Haumea, Makemake, and Eris.

Dwarf planets share two traits with planets. They **orbit** the Sun, and they are round in shape. However, unlike a planet, a dwarf planet has not cleared the area around its orbit. In other words, a dwarf planet shares its region of space with other objects.

Makemake

Eris

DWARF PLANET
Facts

Pluto

Haumea

Size

Dwarf planets are smaller than any of the planets in Earth's solar system.

Pluto

Pluto was once thought to be the ninth planet from the Sun. Today, Pluto is known as a dwarf planet, and there are eight planets in our solar system.

The Future

Scientists believe that there are many more dwarf planets yet to be discovered.

Naming Dwarf Planets

When Pluto was discovered, people from all over the world suggested names for it. Venetia Burney, an 11-year-old girl from England, suggested the name Pluto, a Roman god. The first two letters of the word Pluto are the initials of the **astronomer** who set up the **observatory** where Pluto was discovered. His name was Percival Lowell.

Ceres was discovered in 1801. At the time, Ceres was thought to be an asteroid, but it was later identified as a dwarf planet. It is named after the Roman goddess of farming. The dwarf planet Eris was first spotted in 2003. It is named after the Roman goddess of discord, or disagreement between people.

Makemake and Haumea

The dwarf planets Makemake and Haumea do not get their names from Roman or Greek mythology.

The name Makemake comes from Rapa Nui **mythology**. Makemake is the chief god in their mythology.

Haumea is named after the Hawai'ian goddess of childbirth. Its moons are named after daughters of Haumea: Hi'aka and Namaka.

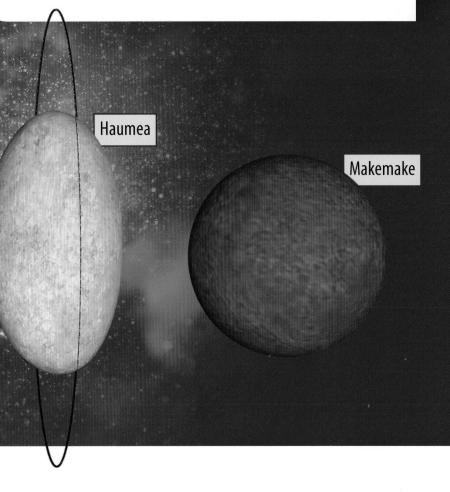

Haumea

Makemake

First Sightings

In 1930, an American astronomer named Clyde William Tombaugh discovered Pluto. At first, it became the ninth planet in Earth's solar system.

In the early 1990s, scientists began to discover icy objects farther out in the solar system than any known planets. An American astronomer named Mike Brown found an object in the **Kuiper Belt.** This object appeared slightly larger than Pluto. It was named Eris.

The discovery of Eris created a problem. Since Eris was thought to be larger than Pluto, many astronomers felt it should be named the tenth planet. Others did not want to make Eris a planet. They believed there could be many objects larger than Pluto in the Kuiper Belt. In order to resolve this problem, a strict definition for the term "planet" was needed.

Pluto was first spotted from the Lowell Observatory in Arizona. The part of the observatory that houses the telescope was later renamed the Pluto Dome.

A New Definition

On August 24, 2006, the **International Astronomical Union (IAU)** held a meeting. At the meeting, they talked about the discovery of Eris.

More than 2,500 important astronomers and other scientists went to the meeting. They decided to give a new definition to the word "planet." This decision meant that Pluto no longer fit the definition of planet.

Eight objects in the solar system fit the IAU's new definition of planet. They are Mercury, Venus, Earth, Mars, Jupiter, Saturn, Uranus, and Neptune.

The IAU held a vote to approve the definition of a planet.

Spotting Dwarf Planets

In 2006, Pluto, Ceres, and Eris were the first objects in space to be called dwarf planets. Since then, two new dwarf planets have been named: Haumea and Makemake.

Astronomers are always searching for new dwarf planets. In fact, they have already found many. At least 100 objects in the solar system could be dwarf planets. However, the IAU has not yet decided these are dwarf planets.

Pluto

Makemake

Eris

See For Yourself

Dwarf planets are simply too small and too far away for people to see just with their eyes. Sometimes, people can see dwarf planets using a powerful telescope. They need to know where and when to look though. Even then, dwarf planets usually appear as just a speck in the sky. Dwarf planets are best viewed from an observatory.

Sedna was discovered in 2003 using a very powerful telescope. Many scientists think Sedna is a dwarf planet.

Dwarf Planets In Our Solar System

Earth's solar system is made up of eight planets, five known dwarf planets, and many other space objects, such as asteroids and **comets**. The dwarf planet Ceres is located between Mars and Jupiter. The other dwarf planets are all located in the outer solar system, beyond Neptune. The dwarf planets beyond Neptune are called "plutoids."

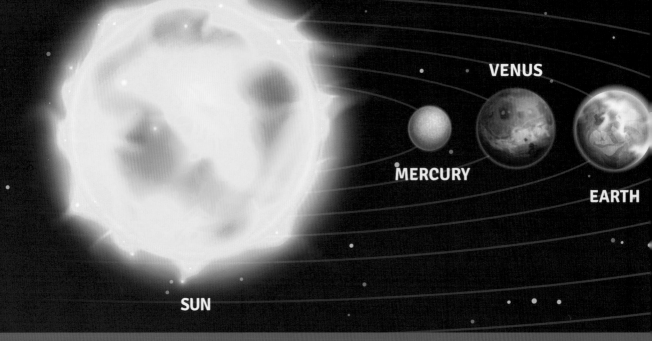

SUN

MERCURY

VENUS

EARTH

Dwarf Planets

A dwarf planet is a round object that orbits the Sun. It is larger than an asteroid or comet but smaller than a planet.

Moons are not dwarf planets because they do not orbit the Sun directly. They orbit planets and dwarf planets.

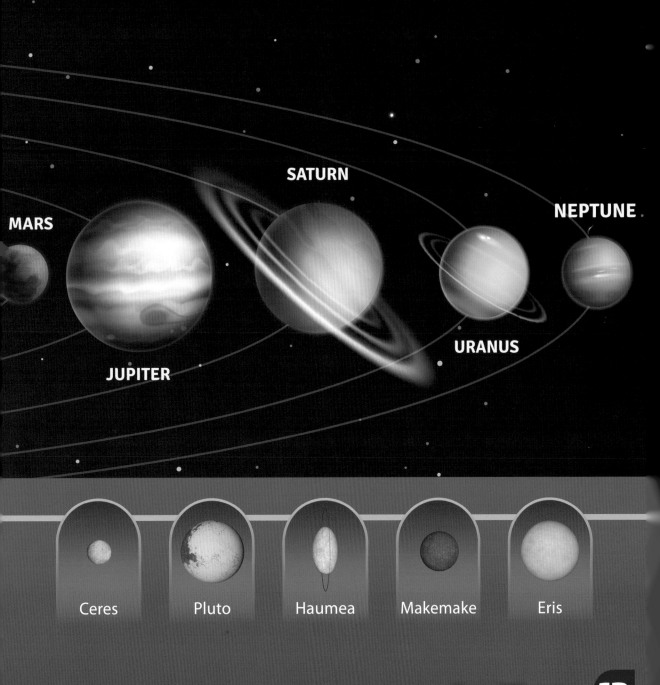

Order of Planets

Here is an easy way to remember the order of the planets from the Sun. Take the first letter of each planet, from Mercury to Neptune, and make it into a sentence. **M**y **V**ery **E**nthusiastic **M**other **J**ust **S**erved **U**s **N**oodles.

MARS

JUPITER

SATURN

URANUS

NEPTUNE

Ceres

Pluto

Haumea

Makemake

Eris

Dwarf Planets and Earth

Dwarf planets are small. The largest known dwarf planets are Pluto and Eris. Scientists today believe Pluto may be slightly larger. Ceres is one of the smallest known dwarf planets, followed by Makemake and Haumea. The dwarf planet Haumea has a unique shape. It is not perfectly round.

All known dwarf planets are smaller than Earth. Earth is about five times bigger around than Pluto.

Pluto's diameter
1,430 miles
(2,302 km)

Earth's diameter
7,926 miles
(12,756 km)

Ceres's diameter
592 miles
(952 km)

Comparing Dwarf Planets

Dwarf Planets (by distance from the Sun)	Distance from the Sun	Years to orbit the Sun	Diameter	Rotation Period	Year of Discovery
Ceres	257 million miles (414 million km)	4.6 Earth Years	592 miles (952 km)	9 hours	1801
Pluto	3,670 million miles (5,906 million km)	248 Earth Years	1,430 miles (2,302 km)	153 hours	1930
Haumea	3,997 million miles (6,432 million km)	285 Earth Years	* 770 miles (1,240 km)	4 hours	2003
Makemake	4,215 million miles (6,783 million km)	305 Earth Years	888 miles (1,430 km)	22.5 hours	2005
Eris	6,326 million miles (10,180 million km)	557 Earth Years	1,445 miles (2,326 km)	25.9 hours	2003

* Haumea is shaped like an egg. Some parts of the planet are wider. Others are more narrow.

Dwarf Planets Today

The Kuiper Belt is in the outer reaches of Earth's solar system. The Kuiper Belt contains icy objects that scientists know very little about. This includes four of the five known dwarf planets in the solar system.

The first spacecraft to ever enter the Kuiper Belt was Pioneer 10 in 1983. It did not visit any objects in the region. In 2006, **NASA** launched the New Horizons probe. It flew by Pluto and its moons in 2015, becoming the first spacecraft to explore the dwarf planet. Since then, the probe has been exploring the Kuiper Belt. Scientists hope New Horizons will find other dwarf planets.

Pioneer 10
Launched 1972
Vehicle Flyby

New Horizons
Launched 2006
Vehicle Flyby

Dawn
Launched 2007
Vehicle Orbiter

Planet Watchers

Clyde Tombaugh discovered Pluto

American Clyde Tombaugh found "Planet X" in 1930. He was only 24 years old at the time of the discovery. As a child, Tombaugh shared his father's interest in the planets. After high school, Tombaugh did not have enough money to attend college. Instead, he worked at the Lowell Observatory.

Tombaugh took photographs of the sky at night. He spent hours looking at the photographs and comparing them with one another. After months of hard work, Tombaugh discovered an object that moved around the sky in a similar way to the planets. Tombaugh had discovered Planet X. Soon after the discovery, Planet X was named Pluto.

Clyde Tombaugh used a large telescope at Lowell Observatory to photograph stars.

Mike Brown discovered Eris and Makemake

Mike Brown is an astronomer and professor at the California Institute of Technology. He has been looking for objects in the Kuiper Belt since 1998.

Brown and his team use a special camera to take digital photographs of the sky. They have discovered a number of notable objects in the Kuiper Belt. Eris and Makemake are the best-known discoveries so far. The team has also discovered 15 other dwarf planets, but these have not yet been confirmed by the IAU.

Mike Brown believes there could be thousands of dwarf planets yet to be discovered.

YOUNG SCIENTISTS AT WORK

How Far to the Kuiper Belt?

Try this activity to see how far the Kuiper Belt is from the Sun compared to Earth.

You will need:
- a large ball
- scissors
- string
- tape

In this activity, the ball stands for the Sun. Pieces of string stand for the distance between the planets and the Sun.

1. Measure a piece of string 2 inches (5 centimeters) long. Cut the string to this length. Place the large ball on the floor. Tape the string to the bottom of the ball. This piece of string stands for the distance from the Sun to Earth.

2. Cut a piece of string 80 inches (204 cm) long. Tape it to the end of the first piece of string. Stretch it out along the floor. Look at the difference between the length of the strings. This represents how far the Kuiper Belt is from the Sun compared to Earth.

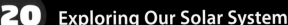

DWARF PLANET
Facts

Gravity

Dwarf planets have enough **gravity** to give them a rounded shape.

Rock and Ice

Dwarf planets are made of rock and ice.

Moons

Dwarf planets can have moons. Moons have been discovered around Pluto, Haumea, and Eris.

What Have You Learned?

1 Dwarf planets can all be found in the Kuiper Belt. True or False?

2 What is the name of the space mission currently exploring the Kuiper Belt?

3 Which dwarf planet is shaped like an egg?

4 How many known dwarf planets are there?

5 What are most known dwarf planets made of?

6 Who first discovered Pluto?

7 In what year did the International Astronomical Union (IAU) change Pluto's status to that of a dwarf planet?

8 Which dwarf planets are thought to have moons?

9 Which two dwarf planets do not get their names from Greek or Roman mythology?

10 Who discovered the dwarf planet Eris?

Answers
1. False 2. New Horizons 3. Haumea 4. Five 5. Rock and ice 6. Clyde Tombaugh 7. 2006 8. Pluto, Eris, and Haumea 9. Makemake and Haumea 10. Dr. Mike Brown

Key Words

asteroids: small, solid objects in space that circle the Sun

astronomer: a person who studies space and its objects

comets: small objects in space made from dust and ice

gravity: a force that pulls things toward the center

International Astronomical Union (IAU): a group of astronomers who make decisions about planets and their features

Kuiper Belt: region of the solar system beyond the known planets

mythology: stories or legends, often about gods or heroes

NASA: National Aeronautics and Space Administration; the part of the U.S. government responsible for space research

observatory: a building with a large telescope

orbit: the nearly circular path a space object makes around another object in space

solar system: the Sun, the planets, and other objects that move around the Sun

Index

AV2

Get the best of both worlds.

AV2 bridges the gap between print and digital.

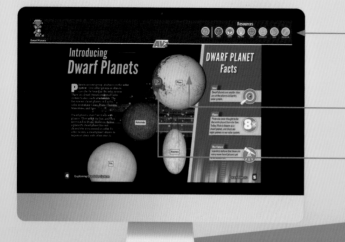

The expandable resources toolbar enables quick access to content including **videos**, **audio**, **activities**, **weblinks**, **slideshows**, **quizzes**, and **key words**.

Animated videos make static images come alive.

Resource icons on each page help readers to further **explore key concepts**.

Published by AV2
350 5th Avenue, 59th Floor
New York, NY 10118
Website: www.av2books.com

Library of Congress Control Number: 2019951409

ISBN 978-1-7911-1724-5 (hardcover)
ISBN 978-1-7911-1725-2 (softcover)
ISBN 978-1-7911-1726-9 (multi-user eBook)

Printed in Guangzhou, China
1 2 3 4 5 6 7 8 9 0 24 23 22 21 20

022020
101119

Project Coordinator: Priyanka Das
Art Director: Terry Paulhus

Photo Credits
Every reasonable effort has been made to trace ownership and to obtain permission to reprint copyright material. The publishers would be pleased to have any errors or omissions brought to their attention so that they may be corrected in subsequent printings.

AV2 acknowledges Alamy, Getty, NASA, Shutterstock, and Wikimedia as its primary image suppliers for this title.